I KEPT MY PROMISE

My PreciousApple Publishing LLC

© Copyright 2021

All rights reserved.

No part of this book may be used or reproduced mechanically, including photocopying, recording, taping or any information storage retrieval system without the written permission of the publisher except in the case of brief quotations embodied in critical articles and reviews.

ISBN: 978-1-7350450-3-0

DEDICATION

This book is dedicated to my amazing mother, Gwendolyn Felder. Mom, I want you to know I was listening and truly cherish all of the times you shared your childhood memories and experiences with me. Like many others, your childhood was not ideal and sometimes painful, but it truly helped mold you into the compassionate person you are now.

I appreciate your commitment and care for family and your griot nature of passing down generational stories and events from your past (like Cousin Hezekiah McDonald Sr.). You have allowed our ancestors' legacy to live on through our casual conversations, and I love you for this.

In writing your story, I compared notes with Kim and TyNathan for accuracy. I am hopeful this book will keep your legacy around beyond our life for our family future generations. Seeing your story in print has allowed me to understand your nurturing and giving nature and how to forgive people who hurt you. I believe you are an amazing woman, and helping so many people sometimes at your own detriment validates this for me.

Sincerely,
Your daughter Kelli

CHAPTER 1

THE FOUNDATION

Gwendolyn Marie was born to Nathaniel and Jean Elizabeth Hall in 1948. She grew up in what is known as the downriver, tri-city area of Southwest Detroit, Ecorse, and River Rouge, Michigan. She had a large, close-knit extended family. Gwen's mother, Jean, had seven siblings: Edwin, Ulysses, Clarence, Dolly Mae, Herbert Lee, Herman, and Gregory. Her father, Nathaniel, had three siblings: Milton, Alice Geraldine, and Carl.

Gwen's family would frequently come together to fellowship over Sunday dinners, summer barbecues birthdays, and various accomplishments family members had achieved. Gwen was the first niece of all her aunts and uncles and her grandparents' first grandchild on both her mother and father's side of the family. This family position meant she grew up with an abundance of love, and every day was like Christmas for her. She did not receive expensive gifts but did get lots of hugs, kisses, and quality time with her family.

Gwendolyn began to be called Gwen by her family members and friends at an early age, because a relative decided Gwendolyn was too old-sounding a name for a young child. Even though she was young, Gwen soaked up everything her grandmothers, parents, aunts, and uncles taught and showed her through their words and actions. She learned at a young age what were acceptable and unacceptable behaviors. Gwen knew to stay away from drugs and alcohol and do well in school and respect her elders like her family told her. There was a history of drug and alcohol abuse on both sides of Gwen's family, so she knew there was a great chance of becoming addicted if she tried those poisons.

CHAPTER 2

THE GRANDMOTHERS

Gwen loved both her grandmothers but the love she had for her maternal grandmother Alice, lovingly called Mother, was exceptional. Gwen worried about Mother because she had terrible asthma and sometimes drank too much. She tried her hardest to see Mother every day to make sure she was okay. During her visits to Mother's house, they would talk for hours as Mother worked around the house cleaning or preparing dinner.

Mother cleaned houses for work, and Gwen wanted Mother to relax when she was at home, so she would always assist with the housework and cooking. Mother was an excellent cook and homemaker. Gwen loved to eat Mother's cooking and see her decorate the house, setting fancy formal dinner tables with cloth napkins, tablecloths, centerpieces, and food that was equally pleasing.

Gwen would watch and help Mother set the table, sew the curtains, reupholster the sofa, and rearrange all the furniture. Whatever project Mother was working on, Gwen was always willing to assist her with it. It did not take long before she knew where to place the salad fork, dinner fork, spoons, saucers, water glass, and napkins on a formal dinner table. Gwen could also wash windows and woodwork at a young age and make them shine like they were brand new.

Gwen really enjoyed when Mother had company come over. She sometimes got to sit and watch Mother play cards and laugh with her friends. Gwen would listen to the grown-ups talk about what was going on in their lives and the neighborhood before being told to exit the room once they noticed she was listening. Gwen knew that Mother worked hard outside and inside her home and often worried about her children, so watching her grandmother laugh and enjoy herself made Gwen smile

One day when Gwen visited Mother, she was disappointed to see Mother sad and crying. Gwen was very concerned and asked Mother what was wrong. Mother explained that she was tired of seeing so many Black people in the community, including Gwen's uncles, mistreated by some police officers.

This was when Gwen promised Mother that she'd become a police officer when she grew up and treat all people with respect and dignity. In return, Mother promised Gwen that she would never take another drink of liquor because she saw how her drinking made Gwen feel.

Cassie was Gwen's paternal grandmother, and everyone called her Big Momma. Big Momma was round, short, and wore cat eyeglasses. She had dark hair with snow-white roots. She was known for many things, and one was always chewing Snuff and spitting it in a small can she kept beside her.

Big Momma loved Gwen, but Gwen thought Big Momma was mean and didn't like her because she looked so much like her mom Jean. She didn't like that Big Momma would often clean the kitchen, wash down the stove, refrigerator, and floor with a dishcloth, and then wipe Gwen's mouth with the same cloth. YUCK!

Jean and Big Momma did not have the best relationship. Big Momma was not ready for Gwen's dad to marry and have a family, so Big Momma would oftentimes mistreat Gwen's mom Jean whenever she could. Despite the bad things Gwen heard Big Momma say about her mom Jean and how she treated Jean, Gwen still loved Big Momma and respected her as she had promised both her parents she would.

There was a garden in Big Momma's backyard that Gwen loved to eat from. Big Momma would have Gwen pick fresh collard greens and other vegetables from the garden daily for lunch and dinner. It was Big Momma who helped Gwen develop her love for greens and cornbread. She loved to eat greens and cornbread with Big Momma because she got to eat them with her fingers instead of with a fork.

The food that Gwen detested the most was chicken, and that dislike came at the hands of Big Momma. One day Big Momma took Gwen to the store. When they got there, t the merchant said, "Baby girl, pick out a chicken." There were several chickens, but Gwen picked the most beautiful bird with bright colors and a lot of agility, thinking this chicken would be her new friend.

After Big Momma paid for the chicken, she and Gwen walked back home, where Big Momma had a barrow of boiling water ready on the back porch. Gwen learned that the chicken she selected was for food and not friendship. She watched Big Momma kill the bird, dip it in the boiling water and pluck off the feathers, which she threw in the yard for the children to chase. Big Momma then took the bird into the house, cut it up, cleaned it up, and fried it up. She then put it on the table and told Gwen and her brother to eat it up.

Gwen could not enjoy the meal because she felt responsible for the chicken's death. She could not make herself eat the once beautiful and living bird she chose to bring home from the store.

During the 1950s, children in Gwen's community did not tell their grandmothers they would not eat their cooking, because they knew they would get a whipping. Gwen's remorse for the chicken and refusal to eat got her a whipping with a switch, and from that day forward, she did not eat chicken.

Other than the greens and cornbread, another treat about visiting Big Momma's house was that Gwen got a chance to spend time with one of her favorite uncles, Uncle Carl. Uncle Carl always spent time talking with Gwen, bringing her gifts, and making her things.

One day Uncle Carl surprised Gwen with a beautiful brown leather purse that he'd made for her. He even put her initials on it, and Gwen loved that purse.

Uncle Carl knew that Gwen was smart, mature, and trustworthy, so he shared with her that he could not read or write very well and wanted to learn how to write his name and read signs he saw when he walked down the streets. He would often sign his name using only the letter X.

Gwen felt special that her Uncle Carl shared this information with her and promised to teach him how to read and write his name. She was only in elementary school herself, but everything she learned in school, she taught to her Uncle Carl.

CHAPTER 3

AT HOME

At Gwen's home, there was just Gwen, her younger brother, Cedric, and their father. Gwen and Cedric were best friends. They were each other's best company. They did not have a television to entertain them, they only had each other. They would play games of checkers and marbles, laugh, and read books together.

When they were allowed to play outside with the other children, their dad told them to come in before the streetlights came on but Cedric would always break the rules. Cedric and Gwen knew they would get a whipping for disobeying their dad. Gwen would always go inside, but Cedric stayed outside and played. He told Gwen the whipping would only last a few minutes, so he would stay out and have more fun. Cedric ended up getting a lot of whippings and always bragged about all the fun Gwen missed by going inside.

Cedric would also read ferociously. People always commented on the fact that Cedric kept reading material with him and invited others to read what he was reading.

Gwen's parents had separated, and her father, Nate, insisted on raising Gwen and Cedric alone, against their mother's wishes. Gwen's mom, Jean, wanted to raise her children, but Nate insisted on caring for them without her. Nate wanted to show others that he could raise his children by himself, especially his daughter.

Jean was young, beautiful, and drew the attention of anyone that crossed her path because of her beautiful, flawless caramel skin, long dark hair, and magnetic personality. Jean's hair was so long she could sit on it.

Everyone wanted to be around Jean because she was fun and pretty, but when Jean married Nate, he wanted that to change. Jean did not like how Nate started to treat her or the way he allowed his mother, Big Momma, to treat her, so she left him. Nate thought Jean would come back to him if he kept Gwen and Cedric, but she never did. Jean wanted her children, but she did not want to be with Nate.

After years of being separated, Jean still made every effort she could to visit her children. Gwen, Cedric, and their father, Nate, lived with Big Momma for a short period of time. Jean knew she could only see her children by going through Big Momma, and Big Momma did not make that easy. Gwen loved her mom and would cry because she had to visit with her mom through the windows of Big Momma's home.

Big Momma refused to let Jean come inside, and she wouldn't let Gwen and Cedric go outside to visit with their mother. That did not stop Jean. Rain or snow, Jean would visit with her children standing outside the window. Gwen and Jean would both cry and put their hands against the window glass to feel closer as they visited with each other.

During one visit, Jean told Gwen that she was having a baby and that Gwen would be a big sister again. Months later, Gwen met her new sister Crystal Lynette. Crystal, or "Stank" as they called her, did not live with Gwen and Cedric, but Jean and her family made sure the children were close.

When Cedric and Crystal were older, they would often tease Gwen about her being so bossy and always telling them what to do, even though she was only a few years older than them.

When Gwen, Cedric, and their dad moved into their own home, their dad took pride in teaching Gwen how to stitch clothes, cook, clean, and behave like a respectable young lady. Nathaniel was a tall thin man. He was Big Momma's oldest son and he took care of his mother and siblings after his father, John Henry, passed away.

Nathaniel was a hardworking man who served in World War II. He was an avid reader and good with numbers. He took a particular interest in the African

diaspora. It pleased him to teach his children about their history.

Nate tried to please everyone. He felt horrible about his wife Jean leaving him, but he felt he could not leave his mother and siblings because they depended on him financially. He also could not afford to pay bills at two households.

Nathaniel once walked to Chicago after hearing about lucrative employment to support his family, but it was in Detroit that he found steady employment, owning and operating fleets of cabs within the City Cab Company.

Nate wanted the best for his children. Even though he did not attend church himself, he made sure Gwen and Cedric were in church every Sunday, starting with Sunday School, as well as attending the morning, afternoon evening services. Both children were also members of the youth choir, on the usher board, in Vacation Bible School, and participated in Easter programs. Gwen was even a member of a gospel group with some of her church friends, and they traveled to different churches and sang.

Nate received an abundance of support for his children from neighbors in his community. Even though there were many women in Gwen's life to give her guidance and helping to rear her, women in her community also embraced her.

Many women in her neighborhood assisted with combing Gwen's hair, teaching her about becoming a young lady, and dressing her for special occasions. One of these occasions was when her dad took her to see Billie Holiday at the Fox Theatre. Gwen marveled at the attention she received regarding her beautiful dress, coat, and hair that day.

Gwen used the things she learned from the women in her life to care for herself, her dad, and her brother. Being the only female in her home, Gwen took charge of mothering Cedric. She cooked and cleaned up after him, combed his hair, ironed his clothes, dressed him, helped him with his homework, and was his best friend when he was bored. Even though he didn't act like he was listening to her and felt she bossed him too much, Cedric actually did listen to her, respected her, and knew that Gwen loved him.

The year Gwen graduated from high school, her neighborhood organized a block party to celebrate their first high school graduates, and Gwen was one of them. When she announced to her father during the block party that she wanted to attend Port Huron Junior College, her dad said, "Gwen, let's focus on your high school graduation right now."

A neighbor overheard the conversation and said, "Oh, she's going to college!" and then proceeded to go around the party taking up a collection for Gwen to go to school. A neighbor even arranged for Gwen to stay with the their aunt, who lived in Port Huron. She completed one semester of college before her dad was laid off, and she was forced to return home.

CHAPTER 4

NEW FAMILY MEMBERS

As the years went by, Gwen ended up with many cousins as her aunts and uncles got married and had children. Gwen babysat her cousins and this is where she learned how to care for babies, comb and braid hair, and comfort children when they weren't feeling well. She even took them to church, movies, plays, and concerts with her own money. She bought shoes and school clothes for them as well.

They called on Gwen for any and everything, and anything she could do to help them, she did. Her cousins, aunts, and uncles that married into her family learned early on that their cousin and niece Gwen was dependable and got things done. With many cousins on her mother's and father's side of her family, there were even more birthdays, graduations, and family celebrations. From the Hall, McDaniel, Wilson, and Warren families, Gwen was surrounded by loved ones who she helped and that helped her.

It was typical for her family to drop by at any time without notice and stay for hours just talking. There did not have to be a special occasion for them to visit; they just enjoyed each other's company.

A few of her aunts and uncles worked for the Big Three Automakers, either Ford Motor Company, Chrysler, or General Motors, so they would often visit each other to show off their new cars and take each other for rides.

CHAPTER 5

GROWING UP

Upon returning home from Port Huron Junior College, Gwen, who valued education, continued her schooling a short time later at Wayne County Community College and then Wayne State University. She earned degrees in English Language and Literature, Criminal Justice, and African Studies.

Gwen met Tyrone Felder, and they had a long courtship that extended during the time Tyrone was in the Vietnam War. Shortly after his return, he and Gwen got married and had two daughters.

When they purchased their first home, Gwen prided herself on decorating with her own unique style of fashion. Tyrone accepted Gwen's unique flair for fashion and decorating. They once had fire engine red carpet, yellow walls, and brown appliances. People often visited their home to see what Gwen's new home décor looked like.

As a mom, Gwen would often dress her daughters alike, and would make the clothes when she wanted Tyrone and herself to have coordinating outfits with the girls. She kept her daughters active with piano, tap and swim lessons, choir practice, Girl Scouts, summer camp,

Upward Bound, and the Detroit Police Explorers. She provided them with every experience she could to make sure they were well-rounded children.

Her daughters say the one thing Gwen did wrong was putting Jheri Curls in their hair. Tyrone, Gwen, and the girls at one point all had Jeri Curls at the same time. They would often argue over who used the most activator when the bottle was empty. She says she thought it was easy maintenance for the family to all have Jheri Curls, but she was wrong.

Gwen, the trendsetter, believed in changing her hair regularly. From the short blond cut, curly wigs, the natural, and locks, she has done it all.

As a homemaker, she regularly updated their home by changing the curtains, carpet, paint, and adding sculptures and pictures. She enjoyed her life as a wife and mother, but she wanted something else to do when her children were in school. So, Gwen joined the workforce at Michigan Bell and later went to Great Lakes Steel as she waited for eligibility with the Detroit Police Department.

CHAPTER 6

KEEPING HER PROMISE

As Gwen's grandmothers, grandfathers, parents, some aunts, uncles, and neighbors passed away, she remembered all the things they taught her and how they made her feel. As a middle-aged adult, Gwen still loved decorating and having family over for holidays with all the holiday décor because it reminded her of good times with Mother.

She earned a reputation for setting beautiful dinner tables and creating ambiance just like Mother did. She also sewed clothes, curtains, bedding comforters, reupholstered her sofas, and rearranged her furniture regularly like Mother once did.

Like Big Momma, Gwen also maintained her love for vegetables. Anyone that knows Gwen knows she is always asking for greens and cornbread, but unlike Big Momma, she now uses a fork when she eats them.

She made a promise to herself to pass on the things she was taught and to take care of her family and community members just like she was cared for. She encourages everyone to avoid drugs and alcohol as her aunts and uncle told her to do. Gwen even put several family members, friends, and neighbors into drug and alcohol treatment centers to help them with their addictions.

Everywhere around, Gwen saw people who needed help and people who helped her. She wanted to make her family proud and let them know they could depend on her. She wanted to keep her promise to Mother and be a good police officer. She wanted to be a teacher and help people like her Uncle Carl, and she wanted to be a good friend and caregiver like she was to her younger brother, sister, and cousins.

Gwen did many of the things she planned on doing as a child and more. Her employment at Michigan Bell as a switchboard operator and then Great Lakes Steel as an Overhead Crain Operator were only temporary positions while she waited to join the Detroit Police Department. Even though she earned more money with Great Lakes Steel, her promise to her grandmother and commitment to her community intensified her desire to be a police officer.

During the 1970s to join the police department, women had to be 21 years of age with two years of college, while men's requirements were different. Men only had to be 18 years old, and needed no college to join the Detroit Police Department. It took a lawsuit against the Department to allow women to join the force with the same requirements as the men.

Gwen fulfilled her promise to Mother and worked in law enforcement for 31 years. She worked five years with the Wayne County Sheriffs as a turnkey and 26 years as a Detroit Police Officer.

Being a public servant, she helped protect Detroit's streets and even provided counsel to inmates while working inside the jail. Every day that Gwen put on her police uniform, she remembered her promise to Mother, "to be a police officer that treated everyone with respect and dignity."

During one of her work shifts, a woman hit Gwen's police car and caused Gwen to have permanent back pain. Gwen went many years, unable to stand up straight and receiving physical therapy. After many years of policing, she retired from the police department due to this severe and continuous back pain.

CHAPTER 7

AFTER THE ACCIDENT

After a few years, Gwen had gradual improvements to her back. She became more mobile and busied herself with helping her family, friends, and community. Unable to work in law enforcement, she loved being involved in the Police Officers Chorale Choir. The Choir was made up of Detroit Police Officers, Wayne County Sheriffs, and other policing agencies that professed their love for Christ and ministered to the community by singing gospel music. The choir's motto was "Badge, Gun, Authority, Nothing without God." Gwen was the business manager and sang with the choir for almost 20 years, where she built treasured friendships and family ties.

She also joined several ministries at her church ranging from the Consolation and Jubilee choirs, Pastor's Courtesy Guild Ministry, Sunday School Ministry, Christian Debutante Ministry, Prison Ministry, Evangelist Ministry, and the Social Justice Ministry.

One great thing that came from not having a job to report to every day was the time she spent with dying family members. Gwen was able to comfort her husband, father, uncles, aunts, and friends that had cancer. She enjoyed spending time with them, taking them to medical appointments, and cooking, cleaning, and caring for them when they could no longer care for themselves. She valued being with them when many of them took their last breath, so they would not die alone. Gwen knew if she were still working for the police department, she would not have been there for her loved ones.

CHAPTER 8

SOCIAL JUSTICE

Gwen also threw herself into social justice issues. The Million Woman March (MWM) was a national call for women across the nation to come together in Philadelphia, Pennsylvania, to unify families. Gwen took the call seriously and opened an office in her neighborhood. In 1997, she registered thousands of women to attend the march. Due to Gwen's efforts, the event organizers reported that Detroit, Michigan registered the largest group of women to attend the rally.

She also helped fill buses and took members of her family and groups of her friends to volunteer in Louisiana in 2005. They helped rebuild houses after Hurricane Katrina destroyed several cities in the state. The Hurricane caused over 1,800 deaths and over $125 billion in damages. Committed to helping people living in Louisiana get on their feet during this devastating time, Gwen learned electrical work, plumbing, and how to install drywall to help restore safe, acceptable housing for Louisiana residents.

Gwen organized another bus trip to Jena, Louisiana, in 2006 after six African-American students were mistreated and placed in jail because they sat under a tree deemed "White students only" at their high school. Gwen filled charter buses with Detroit community members who also felt it was important to stand up against racial injustice by protesting and letting the families of the students know that they had the support of people across the nation.

Gwen's additional social justice projects included taking others to the Dr. Martin Luther King Jr. monument and President Barack Obama's inaugurations. Gwen also sponsored several men to attend the first and 20th Anniversary of the Million Man March.

CHAPTER 9

KEEPING BUSY

A favorite pastime of Gwen's has been helping people create memories. Gwen loves arts and crafts. She shines making candy trees and cups, designing clothes, heritage quilts, hand printed pillows, decorating neighborhoods for the holidays, coordinating weddings, repasts, Mother's Day events, tea parties, and other events for friends, families, and strangers free of charge. She is not technology savvy, but she creates polished and professional obituaries, wedding and family reunion programs, in addition to badges and event paraphernalia to make events special.

Gwen even tried her hand at writing plays. *The Prodigal Son* first, then *The Prodigal Daughter* were two of her favorite productions. She had scenery built, assembled a cast, and performed her production at several local churches.

Whatever project Gwen busies herself with, she still makes time to help others. For several years Gwen drove across town to get her grandchildren off to school, as well as taking them to doctor's appointments and attending almost all school and extracurricular activities they were involved in: basketball, soccer, choir, oratorical competitions, you name it, she was there. She even volunteered at their schools and attended field trips with them. Being a supportive grandmother, she would regularly bring snacks and gifts for her grandchildren and their teammates and choir members to increase their play and fellowship time.

Gwen helped several children, adults, and even families, by taking them into her home when they did not have a place to live. Paying utility bills for family, friends, and strangers in need is something she also regularly does. In addition to time and love, she has gifted many people with legal advice, money, and other resources to improve their quality of life. If she hears of a problem, she is quick to assist without informing anyone of her deeds. She just does it.

For years during the summers, Gwen would often pile her car with her kids, grandkids, and their friends to take them to church functions and the latest movies, plays, or summer events. In the winter, Gwen often gives rides to people walking in inclement weather. She always has hats and gloves in her car to pass out to anyone needing them during cold Michigan winter months.

She has sent several neighborhood kids and family members on college tours, on out-of-state school field trips, enrolled others in educational programs, and fed and clothed those in need. During the Co-Vid 19 Pandemic in 2020, when medical doctors recommended that seniors stay home, Gwen volunteered to deliver food to those in need, took people to the polls to vote, took some to doctor's appointments and grocery shopping too.

CHAPTER 10

YOU AIN'T NO MOTHER TERESA

Once Gwen's father told Gwen that she was no Mother Teresa and that she couldn't help everyone. Mother Teresa was a nun and missionary worker that devoted her life to caring for sick and poor people. Nate thought that Gwen was too nice and let people take advantage of her. He was very protective of his only daughter and did not want to see her hurt.

Gwen responded by saying that she knew she was not Mother Teresa but that she is her brother's keeper and believed she was supposed to help anyone who needed help. Gwen told her dad she has the same beliefs as Dr. King; and felt if she can help somebody as she passes along, if she can cheer someone with a word or a song, if she can show someone they are living wrong, then her living will not be in vain.

Nate loved his daughter and knew that she had a big heart. He accepted Gwen as she was but always tried to protect her from people he thought had bad intentions.

CHAPTER 11

TODAY

Currently, Gwen is alive and well living in Detroit, Michigan. She is the proud mother of two daughters and four grandchildren. She is still very active in her community and in the lives of those she loves. She busies herself doing work for the church, advocating for social justice issues, on Zoom prayer lines, watching her soap operas, playing Scrabble, hosting events, delivering Meals on Wheels, and providing support to seniors and disabled community members. She is appreciative of life and her experiences.

Gwen understands that neither her childhood nor her relatives were perfect, but she accepts her life and experiences for what they are. Her ability to handle her family with compassion and care makes working with the community easy. Gwen is a woman of integrity who does exactly what she says she will do. She has a proven track record of being compassionate, giving, talented, and always keeping her promises.

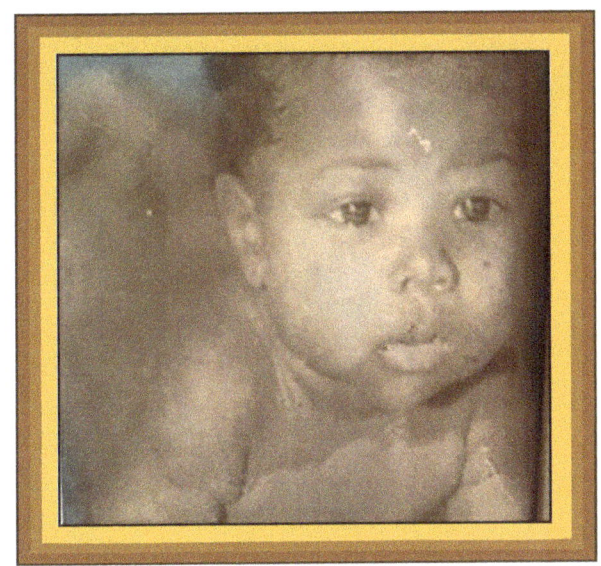

Baby Gwen

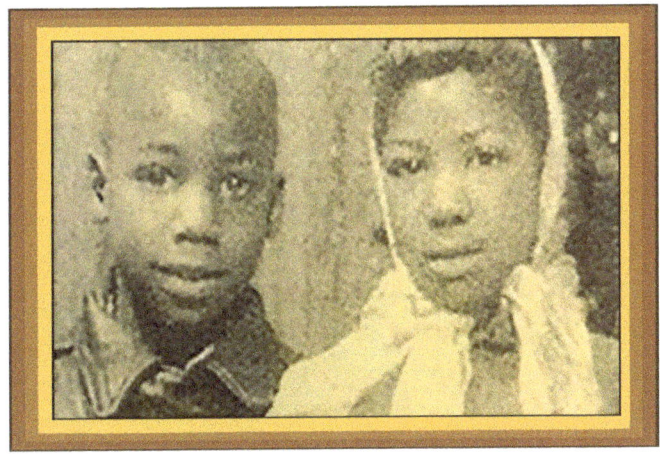

Cedric and Gwen

"It's really not about the numbers... it's about how we'll treat each other when we get back home to Detroit."

GWENDOLYN FELDER, Detroit coordinator for the Million Woman March

www.ingramcontent.com/pod-product-compliance
Lightning Source LLC
Chambersburg PA
CBHW042131100526
44587CB00026B/4253